The Infinite Intoxication of Longing

The Infinite Intoxication of Longing

108 Pieces
of Transcendental Poetry
and A Poetics

JAN ESMANN

RESOURCE *Publications* · Eugene, Oregon

THE INFINITE INTOXICATION OF LONGING
108 Pieces of Transcendental Poetry and A Poetics

Copyright © 2024 Jan Esmann. All rights reserved. Except for brief quotations in critical publications or reviews, no part of this book may be reproduced in any manner without prior written permission from the publisher. Write: Permissions, Wipf and Stock Publishers, 199 W. 8th Ave., Suite 3, Eugene, OR 97401.

Resource Publications
An Imprint of Wipf and Stock Publishers
199 W. 8th Ave., Suite 3
Eugene, OR 97401

www.wipfandstock.com

PAPERBACK ISBN: 979-8-3852-2510-1
HARDCOVER ISBN: 979-8-3852-2511-8
EBOOK ISBN: 979-8-3852-2512-5
VERSION NUMBER 07/25/24

Poetics of Transcendental Poetry

BRIEF PREMISE: THE FOUR TROPES

Rhetorically, we usually recognize four major tropes:

Metaphor

A figure of speech that makes a comparison between two things that are fundamentally different and involves a transfer of meaning from one to the other.

Metonymy

A figure of speech in which one word or phrase is replaced by another to which it is closely related. As with the metaphor, it involves a transfer of meaning from one to the other.

Synecdoche

A figure of speech in which a part is allowed to represent the whole or vice versa.

Irony

A figure of speech where words are used in such a way that their intended meaning is different from the actual meaning of the words.

Here we will deal with the phenomenon of transfer of meaning. In this respect, metonymy can be considered a kind of "sister" to metaphor. Synecdoche is not included because it is a trope that gets its meaning from its own context. Irony is irrelevant.

A METANOETIC POETICS (TRANSCENDENTAL POETRY)

In the following, I first take the classical theory that metaphor is the essence of poetry and discuss its validity. Basically, this means Aristotle and I. A. Richarrds. Later, I try to add another and higher dimension to the debate.

I have not dealt with academic metaphor theorists such as Lakoff, Johnson and Turner. Not because I think Aristotle and Richards have said the last interesting thing, but rather because so much has been said. Moreover, because all metaphor theory is essentially based on the basic assumptions outlined by Aristotle and Richards.

My first working definition of metaphor (meaning transfer in the broadest sense) is therefore as follows:

> *That an unusual meaning is invested in a word, phrase, sentence, etc. that seems "peculiar" in its immediate context, and that this peculiarity invites an unusual meaning to be invested in the word, phrase, sentence or whole.*

If we want to understand artistic quality, and not just poetic rhetoric, it is not very important to determine the forms and functions of metaphor. This is because the metaphor as a transfer of meaning is not present in the poem as a work of art, but in the reading as a reduction of the poem's artistic qualities. Let me explain...

ARISTOTLE'S METAPHOR WORSHIP AND MORASS

Aristotle's determination of the peculiarity of poetic language to metaphor, and his determination of metaphor as the transfer of meaning from one noun to another noun, still carries so much weight (if we extend it from mere nouns) that we must start with his considerations.

Aristotle was hardly original, but merely formal, when he defined metaphor as the transfer of meaning from one noun to another. However, we will not deal with Aristotle's restriction of metaphor to nouns or his other simplifications in the name of early systematization, but rather with the little phrase that he does not explain himself, but which supposedly contains the whole essence of metaphor: *transfer of meaning*.

Contrary to Aristotelian literary theory, we would argue that the essential aspect of metaphor as a poetic functional element, as a trope, is not the transfer of meaning. This is because the transfer only occurs at the moment when the metaphor ceases to be interesting.

In other words: In relation to reception theory, Aristotle's definition is a step too late, so to speak, and only concerns the poetic turn that is becoming a cliche. When the transfer of meaning is complete, we have a cliche. Just look at this banal sentence:

> *Darling, you're the apple of my eye!*

Of course love is blind, but the lover is unlikely to have an actual apple in his eye, and if he does, he probably won't be in love with it. Here the transfer of meaning is so complete that a literal reading seems comical. Here the metaphor has become a cliche.

Aristotle himself must have been aware that his determination of the essence of poetry into tropes was more trivializing than enriching, as he immediately sets up criteria for good and bad metaphors. With these patchwork solutions, he tries to cover up the inappropriateness of his definition. He achieves nothing more than to cover his purely formal rhetorical definition of the distinctiveness of poetic language with a set of values and has not enriched the understanding of poetry as an art in the least. He has merely repeated the usual cliché: Some poetic works are better than others, and the quality depends on the genius of the poet.

He has enriched the understanding of poetry as a rhetorical craft a great deal, but that is completely irrelevant here. All in all, he has merely provided a pseudo-formal basis for justifying norms for good and bad metaphors.

Aristotle's determination is in fact not a determination of the poetically effective and the poetic genius, but only of the poetically worn trope, which is characterized by transferring meaning. But it is not a determination of the talent capable of soaring above the limits of the cognitive possibilities of ordinary consciousness, nous.

In our eyes, this field: *metanous* (i.e. beyond, *meta-*, the ordinary consciousness, *nous*) is precisely the field where artistic genius begins. Aristotle was a noetic, a worshipper of reason, not a metanoetic (a field that inherently cannot be determined semiotically). His definition of the nature of poetry and poetic talent therefore reduces art and genius to a question of talent for rhetorical formalities. There is nothing transcendental in Aristotle at all. There is no such thing as *meta-*. Only *nous*.

We will point out that, in our experience, the presence of this metanoetic void characterizes those works of art (poems, paintings, etc.) that possess the extraordinary, which, in a romantic turn of phrase, can be called genius. We will now call it the metanoesis of the artist/poet/etc. and talk about *metanoetic poetry*, or in simpler terms: *Transcendental poetry*. So where does *meta-nous* come from?

SHORT EXCURSION INTO THE GOSPEL OF MATTHEW

"Μετανοειῦτε η'γγικεν γαἄρ ηᾶ βασιλειῆα τωῃν ουἄρανωῃν." (Matt.4:17)
[*Go beyond the mind, for there is the kingdom of heaven*].

This line is commonly mistranslated as follows: "Repent, for the kingdom of heaven is at hand", where "repent" is a mistranslation of Μετανοεῖῦτε (metanoeite) as "think [noeite] in new [meta-] ways" (i.e. *repent*). But in contrast to this highly tendentious and completely wrong translation, the Greek text is more accurately translated: "Go beyond [*meta*] the mind [*nous*] for here is the Kingdom of Heaven."

It is important to establish the fact that mystics of all cultures have recognized and described for thousands of years: that the "Kingdom of Heaven" (to preserve the reference to the quote) can only be found in radical transcendence, where one finds the ultimate pure being beyond (*meta*) the reason and self-understanding (*nous*) of everyday consciousness.

The metanoetic project and transcendental poetry

We believe that this metanoetic project can help us understand artistic quality and not just the possibilities of metaphor, and ironically (despite millennia of metaphor worship), why metaphor is precisely what reduces the artistic qualities of the artwork to purely rhetorical competencies. Aristotle has emphatically paved the way for this.

Of course, there are many other types of metaphor besides Aristotle's transfer of meaning from noun to noun, such as the genitive metaphor, the verbal metaphor, etc. In addition, there are sentence metaphors that operate at the level of meaning complexes, and the lesser-known, but no less significant, thematic metaphors. However, all these differentiations are not of interest now. Our purpose is to go beyond the rhetorical metaphor field (which is limited to nous).

Aristotle's definition of metaphor as the transfer of meaning is still largely valid. It is valid to the extent that, as is common practice, we let the transfer of meaning be the essential thing, and not the objects (nouns) of the transfer of meaning. The problem is not the rhetorical definition of the metaphor as a trope, because it is subject to purely formal (noetic) criteria. The problem is that it does not necessarily apply to artistic quality.

When Aristotle makes this move of meaning from rhetorics to poetics, he also commits a metaphorization of the very field of meaning he seeks to clarify: poetic genius as a metaphor for rhetorical genius. In doing so, he achieves nothing more than a reduction of one field to another.

Aristotle makes an overlooked mistake when he says that the essential feature of poetic language is metaphor. Metaphor is, of course, a feature of poetic language because it is a feature of all language as such. The metaphor is a trope, something he takes from the stylistic descriptive apparatus of rhetorics and therefore it is not an essential feature of poetry, but rather a general linguistic relation of meaning. Metaphor can be considered a feature of good poetry—and also bad poetry. In fact, a text filled with bad metaphors is more hideous to read than a text that lacks metaphors.

There are poems whose power cannot be understood through metaphor. For example, Basho's (1644–94) haiku. I will render one as follows (without respecting the 5-7-5 form of a regular haiku):

In my new clothes
this morning;
another person

Why this little poem is enchanting is not so easy to explain. As a metaphorist, you have to resort to sentence metaphors and/or thematic metaphors instead of word metaphors, allowing the entire poem to be a metaphor for either time and change or for the identity-creating power of clothing: It's morning, and with the poet's new clothes, a new identity is dawning. You might feel a certain "Aha! that's what the poem is about!" Maybe; read the poem again:

In my new clothes
this morning;
another person

Answer honestly whether the poem, with the metaphorical reading in mind, has lost its enchanting character and become banal.

Since the metaphor has not disappeared because we have identified it, we must conclude that the metaphor is not the active element that lifts the poem to its enchanting height, but rather something that pulls it down from that height. Or consider another famous haiku by Basho (with respect to the form):

> *An old quiet pond . . .*
> *A frog jumps into the pond.*
> *Splash! Silence again.*

Finding metaphors in this beautiful poem seems rather far-fetched.

So Aristotle was wrong. Metaphors can take poetry out of formal logical language and into the world of refined rhetoric, but not into the world of art. There are bad metaphors. So what separates a good metaphor from a bad one? That can only be determined by turning to the potential transcendence of metaphor. Its *metanoetics*.

If we read Aristotle's definition of metaphor as the essential element of poetry (i.e. as a definition of the essential rhetorical element of poetry), then we must agree with him. But when he then attempts to define metaphor, and thus attempts to define poetry as art, he defines nothing more than the mechanism that characterizes the transition from the presence of an enchanting quality in a good poem to the loss of that quality in banal transfers of meaning.

The transfer occurs in the reading and therefore exists exclusively in the reader's head, his nous. This is *immanent poetry*, not *transcendental poetry*.

While it is true that a poetic text invites the reader to make more or less given transfers of meaning, we will not focus on this invitation, as it is a purely rhetorical and reception-theoretical matter. Instead, we will point out the following:

> *The transfer of meaning is not concretely present in the poem, but lies in the encounter between different sets of meanings in the reader's nous, which enables the possibility of metanous.*

In the poem, the metanoetic is located in this field, not in the encounter between one set of meanings and another, but in the free space between the two. It is a field of non-meaning present in the text that we can rightly call *transcendental*. The presence of these transcendental fields characterizes a good poem. Bad poems have none.

This presence of the transcendental is, of course, related to the essence of true mysticism. We will not argue that mystical realizations can be achieved by reading poetry or looking at paintings (an erroneous assumption by the likes of Kandinsky, Malevich and Rothko, which the 20th century has emphatically disproved). Instead, we want to draw attention to a phenomenon that can help us determine the artistic distinctiveness that separates art from craft and poetry from rhetoric. So we are left with these two controversial theses:

1. *Metaphor as a transfer of meaning is not present in the poem as a work of art, but in the reading as a reduction of the poem's artistic qualities to a purely rhetorical phenomenon.*

2. *The metaphor as a linguistic idiosyncrasy potentially opens the text to the reader's field of cognition beyond his or her ordinary field of cognition. At least as a meta-semiotic clue. This is metanoetic and carries the poem's artistic quality.*

RICHARDS AND THE PECULIAR PHRASE

In contrast to Aristotle, I.A. Richards got closer to the matter without actually getting to the essentials. His gain was to point out that it was the words that seemed peculiar in the context that were essential, and that these were the carriers of the transfer of meaning.

So the trope is still essential. But the peculiarity of the distinctive word (or phrase) is now given autonomy, although *peculiarity* as such is not further defined. It is merely postulated to be the carrier of the metaphor. We must now keep this (i.e. the distinctive, or peculiar, phrase) in mind.

Wherein lies the peculiarity? And are there different functional types of peculiarity in the words or phrases that can carry metaphors? Richards' study suffers from the shortcoming that he does not examine peculiarity as something unique and perhaps even highly significant.

Instead, he sees peculiarity as produced by semantic displacement, in relation to the context, that allows a different meaning to be invested. In other words, Richards sees the metaphor as having a dual nature between what he calls *vehicle* and *tenor*. *Tenor* is the element to which properties are attributed. *Vehicle* is the object whose properties are borrowed. Richards thinks something like: The strange word (or phrase) carries the meta-meaning of the poem.

Again, we must point out that while the strangeness of the peculiar word allows it to be a metaphor (or other trope), it is not clear whether this carrying of metaphorical meaning is the artistic function of the strange phrase, or whether it reduces the artistic function of strangeness to a stylistic function. We therefore still have the possibility that the metaphor as a transfer of meaning is not present in the poem as a work of art, but in the reading as a rhetorical manipulation of the reader's nous.

The problem is not that metaphor cannot be delimited—and never has been, if we are to believe Quintillian's remark that the definition of tropes has always given rise to wild debates between literati as well as between literati and philosophers. Without entering into such debates, we can only point out that the problem of metaphor has grown to such an extent that today we must consider whether all cognition is not metaphorical. Not only that, but we must consider whether all cognition is in fact a series of metaphors upon metaphors upon metaphors, and that consciousness, perception of reality, and language are so interwoven that it is impossible to determine whether one is a metaphor for the other.

But perhaps metaphors are not at all relevant to the nature of art, and thus not at all relevant to our case now—even though Aristotle and the entire tradition of Aristotelian literary theory believe that good metaphors cannot be learned: "*This is the mark of genius. For the right use of metaphor means having an eye for similarities"*. Now, I would argue that the mark of genius is not to make one's linguistic statement look like a statement about something else, thereby producing a poetic language of some complexity. (The validity of this is by no means to be denied here. It's just not complete.)

We arrive at the following:

> *The hallmark of poetic (and all other artistic) genius is to have the artwork suggest the metanoetic in ontological vacant spaces.*

Note that the metanoetic is, of course, quite different from non-meaning or meaninglessness, because meaninglessness is a presence that blocks other meaning. "Transcendental meaning", on the other hand, opens up for a hint of other meaning. Or para-semiotic cognition, if you will.

Metaphor is the reader's filling of these peculiar places with meaning transferred from something else in their nous. Metaphor-interpretation is thus the death of transcendental meaning. It is what kills the enchantment of a good poem. It closes instead of opens the moment it is filled. This is not inherent to the metaphor itself, but happens through the reading and the reader's projection of meaning onto the peculiarity of the metaphor.

Metaphor as such is thus the death of non-meaning and a reduction of the artwork from metanoetic to noetic. To put it simply: To a language game.

MEANINGLESSNESS VS. NON-MEANING

The problem of meaninglessness versus non-meaning requires some elaboration. These places of non-meaning usually become carriers of other meaning and thus metaphors or carriers of tropes by virtue of their peculiarity. Meaninglessness, on the other hand, cannot carry other tropes without seeming forced and contrived. Randomly composed words, even from grammatically appropriate categories that meet formal syntactic requirements, rarely produce anything but meaninglessness, at most random meaning. Nor do the "oddities" of such sentences carry Richard's metaphors. So there is something else at stake in the artistically functional (and not just tropically, semantically or linguistically functional) *peculiarities*. Or rather than "at stake": a non-game.

Thus we arrive at the following paradigm:

> *Only by the game not being present, where space is simultaneously set aside for a game and the game is expected to be, can places of metanoetic para-meaning emerge.*

THE PARADIGM OF TRANSCENDENTAL POETRY

In general, for the sake of simplicity, we will refer to para-meaning as non-meaning. Meaninglessness is itself a game—a game defined by negating established rules. In transcendental poetry there are no rules, we are outside the field of reason and mind and inside the metanoetic.

There should be no doubt that poetic reading is a game of meaning, where meaning plays with meaning. Or that metaphor becomes interesting precisely because it plays with the surrounding language game. Metaphor plays a trick on us by replacing the meaning we expect from the familiar with another meaning—and not just from the surrounding language game. In this way, metaphor plays against the surrounding game. Not with it.

The prerequisite for the metaphor to play a different game within such an ambient game is well known: Namely, that the metaphor's peculiar game of meaning "interferes" with the surrounding game of meaning. No matter how different the two games of meaning are, metaphor always requires some kind of semantic relation that presupposes and enables the transfer of meaning. And the transfer of meaning is simply one language game being transferred to, and appearing in, another game. This is assuming that another meaning is introduced into a phrase that functions in a foreign context and is therefore peculiar.

Richard's gain is to point out that this peculiar place in poetic language is not produced by metaphors, but carries metaphors. In other words, he points out that there is something that precedes metaphor without getting closer to determining it.

We will point out that here, in the presupposed, there is a presence of transcendental non-meaning, as opposed to the presence of meaninglessness. The presence of meaninglessness does not in itself allow for the introduction of a new, context-free language game. Anyone can write a meaningless text. It is non-meaning as an opening to the metanoetic that is crucial. Without it, a text without meaning is simply foolish.

If you try to turn a meaningless word or expression into the carrier of a metaphor, the result is usually quite pathetic and poor. It takes a lot of work to argue that the postulated metaphorical meaning is not just continued meaninglessness.

You can argue that the meaninglessness carries metanoetic meaning, but that doesn't change the game because it's nonsense. There are no metanoetic metaphors, only metanoetic non-meaning. We are not surrealists, and the only meaning the meaningless can carry is that of the unconscious. That is *sub-nous*; we go for *meta-nous*.

On the other hand, we find a place of potential transcendental meaning where an oddity occurs that stops the ongoing language game and does not easily establish a new one. Such places are open places where the investment of a *metanoetic hint* can take place.

TRANSCENDENTAL POETRY

The important thing is that the established game is suspended by the peculiarity. At the same time, something emerges that transcends meaning. Semiotics is thus suspended. By being placed in this particular peculiarity, no game is carried, and thus the peculiarity is a place without meaning. The meaning of the word, the phrase, the sentence, the theme, in fact its own meaning, is thus suspended and non-meaning becomes present. At least as a hint.

Non-meaning can thus be understood as the peculiarity that gives the poetic work artistic power and can make language and other works of art enchanting.

This also makes it clear that the moment the non-meaning is made the carrier of a trope (metaphor or anything else), we have eliminated the non-meaning by replacing it with the transferred meaning. This leads back to the point that the metaphor as a transfer of meaning is not present in the poem as a work of art, but in the reading as a reduction of the artistic qualities of the poem.

It should be clear that non-meaning as transcendental meaning, not substitution of meaning, is a valid criterion of artistic quality in the particular places of the poem.

Therefore, we can speak of *transcendental poetry* as a valid poetic genre. Also called *metanoetic poetry*.

108 Metanoetic Poems

Oh! Of the beginning.
Sex and burnt hogs
In my genes of noetic impurity.

Oh! So slow. The Monkey Darwin.
Freud the cigar. Coitus illuminati.

Two great spermatozoa of fluid aporia.

In these fluid moments,
Where I see myself
Reflected in a small creek.

In these fluid moments,
Where I rest motionless
In a restless emptiness of time.

Where on our plains stands
The mountain I always climb?

You hide in its shadow.

Between the moment and eternity
There exists nothing but
A language, without words or signs,
That only absence understands.

A naked attempt to strip life bare
Breathes in the folds of cherry blossoms.

How strange that I sit
With my back against the trunk.

Here I seek a
Non-place of meaning.

Silent in trans-bliss.
Nothing, that separates me and THAT,
Finds admission here.

For those, who do not comprehend,
Everything is a black darkness
They delude themselves is happiness.

When a heart breaks,
[/krək/]

    It sounds like
    A fertilized egg
    Dropped on a floor of

Crystallized yearnings.
[/splət/]

If I had only a single breath,
It reflected the longing of rivers.

And if I had only a single day,
I would still flow in eternity.

Non-created caresses have filled
My lungs with homesickness.

The days struggle in vain.
The drowning death in my cosmos.

Blissful oceans within me

    Overflow,
    Where everything is
    So secret, that

I have forgotten.

Meetings we didn't expect to have,
Await us in those mines,
We dare not enter into.

Those we long for,
Watch over us like
Invisible blood transfusions.

Between the two swings the face
We see in mirrors and sooted caresses.
Me? I am the silver of mirrors and the soot of mines.

I am the blood. I am the syringe. I am Lazarus.

Finally, I have crossed
Storm-filled oceans.

The lighthouse of my spine.
My brain of light.

They navigated me across
The gales of love.

Between the caresses
We didn't comprehend,
And the words
We touched each other with,
Flows a meeting
Of farewell and kisses.

> Our love resembles a city
> Painted by Filoktet.
> *(Antonio di Pietro Averlino.)*

Between the words
We remembered for too long,
And the caresses
That forgot themselves,
We abandon a city
Of geometric dreams.

Lily of the Valley

The grace of the name is mystical.

Jan is a wanderer
In a map of petals.

Guide in sublime love
Leads him to the pollen
He meditates upon.

Oh! To sacrifice one's petals
In an invisible homas fire.

Jan is disintegrated pollen.

I myself am a Lily of the Valley.

A child's cry points in the twilight
Towards dreams, old age and death.
The metamorphosis of wisdom
Behind closed windows and oblivion.

Love screams in the yard,
Mocking the worn-out insights.
Jan is the child's cry and the love.

Living as echoes among the dead.
A child, that is mummified.

Resin and philosophy.

A quiet tremble in the inner sense
Leads Jan into his death:

Like a cool Chablis.
Oh, to get drunk on darkness!

Meanwhile, I sit here
And become drunk with death-bliss.

When I embrace you
With my loves rose,
You feel my thorns.

Am I good enough for you?
Your drops of blood.

Signatures.

The last runes of the year.
Gray homesickness moved in.

The cycle of time measures itself
With drops of insight
In my sentimental nakedness.

When everything collapses in my longing,
Everything returns to its source.
This morning I sat in the park.

I watched people walk their dogs.
Two dogs sniffed each other's butts.

They were happy. I almost understood them.

All my life
I have paddled a kayak
On a frozen lake.

Hope lies beneath me,
Like a frozen nymph.
She observes me.

The mummified saint
Whispers about love
While his body
Becomes more and more transparent.

The invisible becomes visible.
Presence and nowhere.

I am cyan bliss.
Jan is bandages and resin.

In the heart: A skull and a fetus,
Writing to each other
Through homeless plasma.

Blue blood in red fountain pens.
We fear the upcoming words,

We have already thought.

Here time lies restless,
And ponders over tomorrow.
Each moment holds significance
For the restless time.

Next night, this place will diminish
A little from Earth.

Cosmos will toss and turn in bed
Like my sleepless body.

Oh, sweet humility
That few know of.

Naked fire. Who is Jan?
A blazing body of time!

> (Jan died in March 2022.
> Or was it August 2021?
> Or March 1979? All three?)

Only the humility remains,
That the few have spoken of —in vain.

In dark corridors of deathly reverence,
Where butterflies wither.

    (Moments we never kissed.)

In dark memories' fear of whispering,
We hear the pulse of the past.
It measures emptiness with echoes
Of butterfly wings.

Oh! To kiss a sacred word:
Butterflywingdust.

    (Moments we never kissed.)

The quivering phallus of longing
Has moved into Jan's spine.

A metanoetic ejaculation.
Transcendental paradise.

Meanwhile, Jan sits
Genderless on his couch.

Spermatozoa of gilded orgasm
Penetrate Jan's shaking brain.

The sunset paints my eye
With heavy, golden washes.

Then the night takes my sight hostage
To show unreadable insight.

Within every moment
Rests the cyan eternity.

Untouchable.
Blissful,

Like when God and I
Get each other pregnant.

My navigational chart has gone in the sea
Along with all of my belongings.

All that remains is a scent
Of beaches borrowed for lovemaking.

In the mirror, I see an eye. With tears.
One enters my mouth,
And tastes of yesterday.
I go for a walk in the local cemetery.

I sit down and ask the tear,
What it longs for.
In cemeteries, one it's okay to cry.

Just not out of homesickness
And longing.

I have no idea who I am
Or when.
Or where.

Here, where no thoughts exist,
Exists only a presence
In the perfection of absence.

When farewell and arrival lose their meaning,
And the presence of absence burns in everything.

All that remains is the pleasure of losing
The stupidity Jan exalted himself with.

Among the meetings we couldn't have,
And the meetings that uplifted us,
Exists a leaden diary
With indecipherable signs.

We have reached for each other
And lost ourselves
In heavy dreams.

Yet we always speak gibberish,
When we talk about love.

Love without an object.

When bliss overpowers
The waves of the sea,
Time fades into a small lake.

I fish for glimpses,
That swim calmly
Between grains of sand and the cosmos.

God does not whisper, but howls
Like storms between my ears.

Blinded by bliss, I do not see
That death is the price for THAT.

Nakedly remember me, when Jan is gone,
And IT has filled his absence.

In the night's forest of sorrowful trees,
Imbecile owls and silly learning,
I appear in glimpses,
That once could be called "now".

Across foolish forests
Circles my luminous moon.

In this moment I sit
On a song of roses
And vanilla scent.

A few moments later,
I sit on thorns
And a snotty nose.

Does restlessness have no end?
If only you could unite in lovemaking.
After all, you're both infertile.

Where on my ways is
The sign I always miss?

You're hiding in a map,
Where no roads are marked.

Hear me now:
I am a shamed grand piano
Playing its requiem.

Hear me now:
I make noise like God
And Jan in a blender.

I'm waiting at the airport
For a dream that never comes.

Stranded I must sleep
On the hard benches of my life.

Why am I in cosmic darkness,
Trapped in an imaginary body?

It cultivates parting and acetic acid,
Like others cultivate mushrooms or sex.

Now the cherubs' swords have flared up.
My guardian angel sleeps and has nightmares.

Cosmos is pumped by my defective heart-valve
Like soot and linseed oil in a mortar.

While waiting for death,
I packed a gift for God:
Pain, sorrow and isolation.
Just like I was given them.

Now I eat God for lunch,
And piss soma in diamond jars.
At the table trans-God sits and drinks.

IT is drinking the gift.
The endless longing.

The infinite intoxication of longing.

A sea of caresses in vain.

My insides dissolve in memories,
Of seas I did not sail.

When noise and silence unite,
That insight shows its face,
Which I portray in vain.

A silence in which
Barking mongrels sound
Like peonies blooming.

Pain can hold one's hands
With such tenderness
That the heart explodes.

Hospital nights sound
Like robots made out of care.

> *Sometimes I hear the dead*
> *Turning in my bed.*
>
> *The sick who were once here*
> *Have left ethereal sighs.*

Meanwhile, the robots chant
Their rhythmic prayers.

Such humility
Is found only in the distance
Between yesterday and tomorrow
And in dilapidated high-rise buildings.

Lost in bliss-fire.

Thus the days take each other
At face value in my inner cathedral.

Unity and parting.
Devotion and powerlessness.
Sacred frescoes on the walls.

Touch my third eye and show me clearly
If it is possible to know if one is insane.

I am a fresco in a cathedral of fire.

To my tea ceremony, the Pope, the priest
And my grandmother were absent.

Agape came as a narcoleptic shadow,
Who fell over and slept in the tea.

A glorious shadow: Immortal,
Gilded and fantastic,
Which the Pope, the priest and my grandmother
Fear like ascetic sacramental wine.

Hugging immortal trees
That resist the plastic idea
That i am Jan Esmann.

I stand in the forrest
And gild a tree
With invisible euphoria.

Beyond the timpani concert of ecstacy
Instrumentless music shows the
Path to moments of cyan timelessness.

Jan is a zombie made of oblivion.
Hidden is the cyan nothing-all where God
Is transcended and from which God is born.

Between cyan blue cherry blossoms
And a shortcut to eternal peace,
I brush my meditation cushion
With the dream of not dreaming.

An incarnation of ultimate love.
No one can bear it without being
Mummified by the Self in a body
Of cherry blossoms and unmentionables.

While the beautiful flowers fall to the ground,
I tap dance a requiem for Jan.

Oh! To be Being in Itself.
Cyan as the timeless eternity.

Will we reach the dreams we haven't
Pasted on refrigerators and mirrors?

In the elastic time between the present and postcards
A copied journey opens up,
Where eternity announces its arrival
And its departure in a trans-semiotic kiss.

In that moment I always lose myself,
And know we could have met,
If you didn't stick postcards
On fridges and mirrors that don't exist.

Jan is the glue. You are the journey. The postcard
We share. Like a memory neither of us has.

Who among the hosts of angels
   (Rilke's hallucinations)
Could show me the insights
That flow in an invisible river?

Where, if I were to seek,
Would I find the cool insight
That flows in a river of fire?

An invisible calling led me
To the ultimate death,
It is to drown in the Self.

In me there is no time. No now.
No zombie intercourse. No I-ness.
Only the metanoetic cyan sky.

And if anyone asks me
How it is. I answer the idiot:
As an incarnation of Mother Mary.

How to tell a pregnant zombie
That the fetus is a putrefactive dreamer
Who sleepwalks like a castrated crown prince.

In my youth I pupated.

Now I am free and
Spread my wings.

They look like a flower
Having an orgasm.

Jan has dreamed
Of barbiturates and painless death.

Behind it all lurks Jan's absence.
Outside, it's raining cybergothic angst
Made of plastic and the pornography of gas-masks.

>*Noise*
>*(!)*

A fervor that transcends itself
Has killed Jan (painfully) into life.

>*Silence*
>*(!)*

Will we reach it before the longing disappears?
Or must we renounce joy
Before devotion and powerlessness unite?

Yet I longed for longing.
The foolish joy of separation.

Stupid fragments of Jan
Miss that which has no reality,
And seeks to be a body.

The bucket Esmann fills with tears.
The dead drink thirsty for the insight
That killed Jan slowly.

In the bucket I see nothing
Mirrored like a vampire
Made of memories and tomorrow.

The forest of unmade dreams
Covers the joys of the days,
Where we always get lost.

One life is not enough to reach THAT,
Life is too long to bother about.

That's why we pick dew from flowers,
And dress in what we are not.

Of me, wine and religions are made.

> My blood is not mine.
> It is the wine of the restless.

The endless intoxication of longing.

In a fog no one can see through,
Tomorrow walks in its eternal sleep,
And struggles with an endless nightmare.

There is no such thing as now. It is
Like a chance meeting
Between a sewing machine and an umbrella
On an operating table.

Le Comte de Lautréamont
However, created in vain
When he wrote it.

Wrote it with the black hole of freedom
In the fountain pen of his cosmic consciousness.

Isidore Ducasse in memoriam.

NOT
HI
NG

Is the blissful origin of the fragmented.
Oh! To be absolutely nothing without death.

Peculiarities are the tombstones of semioticians.
Oh! To be a meaningless word:

Kamelåså

A time lapse didn't hit me,
But dissolved Jan into moments,
That don't exist.

Me? I am the result
Of the copulation of death and life.
I, non-Jan, am their endless orgasm.

What does not end has no beginning.

Unlike the sentence,
Which at any time is nonsense.

An impotent old man's
Viagra-dreams
About schoolgirls.

The ferryman received his coin and does his job.
He doesn't see that Jan doesn't exist,
Accustomed as he is to transporting corpses.

I am Styx. I am Kali.
Just a drop of sweat in the heatwave of hell,
Where Jan and the cosmos collide.

Splintered in the silence of the Godencounters void
I crumble among the gravel of the sidewalk.
Zombies dance by.

Beyond the ecstasy's timpani concert
Instrumentless music reveals
A path to a presence of nothing in time.

Bliss makes me resemble
A cadaver resurrected
In the orchestra of surrender.

Jan is a bacterium.
I, on the other hand, am a virus
From the past's encounter with tomorrow.

An immortal virus
Awaits in a now,
That does not exist.

Our pursuit of IT
Is dirt on a mirror.

Wipe it off.

The body is a bag of piss and shit
As well as blood, bones, and flesh
And a little bit of mucus and brain matter.

Now my bag sails
On the dreams of happiness,
Resting in everything's ocean.

Stuffed seagulls
Scream about the bag's demise.
Kapok and farewell behind eyes of glass.

With burning hands I now write
A letter to the suitors of twilight.

The night knows no visiting hours,
But bursts into flame when longing is eternal.

Small changes with big ambitions
Cover my life like dust.

I sweep it away
With a broom of sorrow.

Overdosed with self-destruction,
Abstinence and lonely music.

My body sings sentimental songs
About the encounter between Jan and the cosmos.

Here are no metronomes. No I.
Only the melancholy of a cello.

A Christ made of plastic.
An angel with chili eyes.
Copulate in the heart of every priest
On a bed of anguish and St. Paul's letters.

Here sits the not-I,
And listens without thinking.

Crying.

In my oneness with IT
I realize that I see nothing
Other than absence.

Oh, I love everyone
As a silent vibration
Of death's meeting with life.

Then. . .

Under the long shadows
From the sun in my brain
The days sleep the sleep of foxes.

The weeds of interrupted dreams
Cover their burrows and passageways,
Where we get lost at first meeting.

Healthy eyes cut by IT
Contemplate their essence.

I see the world as it is
With my all-seeing blind eye,

Everything is me, though,
Where Jan doesn't exist.

A single life is not enough to achieve THAT,
Life is too long to bother about.

Out of spite, we build uninhabitable towers,
And create gardens no one will enjoy,

Just to give the body the eternity
We ourselves do not have time for.

I live in a park without benches,
Where midnight eats a midnight snack
With Symeon, Juan and I.

Cyan night snack. A meeting
Between the midday light and midnight
In the shadow of my emptiness.

Our search led us
To chambers of silent testimony
Of the relationships we did not enter
Despite the dictates of the body and the hour.

Meanwhile, we must keep searching
For the meaning that does not exist

The dark happiness of emptiness writes
Quirky sentences in ink on black.

I burn charred traces
Across the impotent signs of writing.

With the freedom of the mountain goat
We stumble across memories.

This is how we meet on empty mountains,
Where the will to harmony
Reflects one's layer of expectation
In the other's face of canyons and peaks.

Beyond the final
    Caress.

A bodiless body of cyan melts
My dream of God. And then:

    NothingAll.

Metanoetic moments
At the shaving mirror.

The cessation of dreams
At metro stations.

Two non-things that cause,
Secret tears in plain sight.

Between those moments,
Where day dreams of night,
And the night describes itself,
I yearn like mad.

In those moments I remember,
The place where my heart once was.

The full moon in my brain.
A simple moment of absence.

Oh! A moment of peace,
Where nothingness and presence meet,
And Jan is transcended.

The delight of absence.
In such moments:

Metanoesis.

Jan is moss on the graves of the dead.
Indeed, the dead have wings of moss,
    (Lorca in memoriam)
But we no longer care to hear that.

Oh, to be as simple as moss
In a forgotten poem of farewell and arrival

Where death copulates with immortality

The air around Jan.
Dissolves him like mist.

Jan is dew on a mirror
Of unfulfilled longing.

I've been in a coma,
And transcended death.

Now I am here on borrowed time,
And barely remember Jan.

A cadaver of love
Caries my sorrow.

Here, among the everyday zombies,
Jan reflects on immortality.

There is nothing left but
That which no zombie understands.

*Oh no! Oh
No! Oh
No!*

How long shall we complain
About the abyssal torments,
That meet us in nightmares.

And yet here we are, where those
Demons, who only seek love,
Plague our night.

Lonely ski tracks
In my everyday life
Of snow covered longing.

In these fragrant moments
Where the shadows of love
Cover my past
Of endless moss.

Oh! Moss in my veins
Of what everyone longed for.

Jan is a spore of perfume.

It can't last long
Before lies commit suicide
In the dreams the world is made of.

Those dreams are red wine
Which Jan got drunk on.

We drink longing.

One Night <=> One Day.

Shadows of the sun
Which is the blood of the soul.

The heart is a cliche,
We're waiting to mummify.

Here there's no time.

3000 dreams, at least,
About copper oxide on Kali
Made of brass and
The longing of icons.

Tears of copper green cum,
The end of fertility,
Sacrificed to my Self
Of endless orgasm.

This is too little
Of ecstasy and unspeakability,
Where everything is crystal
And nothing exists.

However, my eye *is*.
It exists. I see
That, which no one sees.

A continuum
Of brackets.

((( )))

TEN SEDOKA

I
I wallowed in bliss
And insight; The companions
Of the encounter with God

I forgot that I
Create the night when the light
Turns in on its very self.

II
Perhaps it is true
That the Beyond must Always
And Ever be beyond Jan.

It must be tested,
Whether time carries itself,
Or is carried by nothing.

III
The moisture and smile
Of the grass does not please me
Where my life has seen itself.

God's morbid game
Plays with itself in my inner
Longing to merge with IT.

IV
If the closed Presence,
We always live, Lives
For itself in everything.

Then a presence
Will be inevitable,
When death kills dying itself.

V
Here the sun is an
Exception in the darkness
That rules the cosmos by far.

In my own body,
Darkness is just a stamp on
What the sun looks like to me.

VI
Send me a greeting,
When you cross the river Styx;
A simple thought is enough.

I will wait for you,
There on the other bank,
For I do live both places.

VII
Perhaps I have
An absence yet to come in
My peace with solitude.

Meeting will be when
All´s burnt into memories.
The ecstasy transcended.

VIII
The reality,
Mind's mother and murderer,
Does not know me any more.

Thus we stand here
Behind all recognition
And joke about each other.

IX
My peaces death by
Stupidity's tyranny
Which no longer rejoices.

The reality
Wanders restlessly in my
Soul waiting for its rebirth.

X

It's how it ended!
Not all at once but spread
Over life upon life.

I pushed Jan so hard;
Often into madnesses.
Now I stand without him ()

Free!

Published books by Jan Esmann

Fiction in Danish

Novel

Nøgent Ego (Naked Ego)

Collections of Short Stories

Strandvaskeren (The Beachcomber)
Drømmefangerne (Dreamcatchers)

Spiritual books in English

The Mystical Theology and Enlightenment (A Kundalini Romance)
Lovebliss
Kundalini Tantra
Enlightenment 101
Handbook for Shaktipat Siddha Yoga Initiates
Poems and Ramblings of a God-intoxicated Yogi
The Secret Tantric Practice: Siddha Shakti Vidya
The Subtle bodies and the Aura

Other books in English

Spirituality and Modern Culture
21st Century Figurative Art
The Artists Craft
The Ultimate Handbook of Psychological Astrology, 2 vols.

Short stories

The Beachcomber
Dreamcatchers

Novel

Naked Ego

www.ingramcontent.com/pod-product-compliance
Lightning Source LLC
LaVergne TN
LVHW051645080426
835511LV00016B/2507